NO ONE EVER TOLD ME

Your Guide to Living Benefits

By Richard Drazien CLU, SRM

NO ONE EVER TOLD ME

America's Best Kept Secret
Living Benefit Life Insurance

Comments from Benefit Recipients

After my husband's heart attack the Living Benefit claim check took care of all our financial worries and let us focus on his getting well.

... *Kathy & Elliott Butler*

Life isn't scripted, but when something like a heart attack happens you do not want to be concerned about money. You want peace of mind and the chance to survive. Living Benefits gave us that opportunity.

... *Sophia & Carlton Dudley*

After I was diagnosed with lung cancer, the Living Benefits claim check allowed me to pay our mortgage, keep current on our bills, and continue our lifestyle.

... *Ronald Webb*

No One Ever Told Me, Your Guide to Living Benefits

Published by Richard S. Drazien (Independent Publisher)
Richard S. Drazien
2208 Windsor Court
Little Rock, AR 72212
rickdraz@yahoo.com

First Edition.
Printed in the United States of America

ISBN 978-1-4675-4612-6

Book design by Good Eye Design, Chris Benzel and Premier Graphics

Table of Contents

Section 3 – The Bonus

Section 4 – Implementation

“There is no end. There is no beginning.
There is only the infinite passion of life.”

… Federico Fellini

“Things which matter most must never be at the mercy of things which matter least.’’

… Goethe

Author's Note

On June 28, 2012 the Supreme Court delivered its decision upholding the Affordable Health Care Act. The debate on what that will mean for Americans and the political efforts to repeal the ruling will continue. As always, it is a fight about power, money, and control, and we are often kept on the sidelines as bystanders to the impact on our lives, be it good or bad.

This book is an attempt to deliver ultimate control into *your* hands.

There are four key elements required for your surviving a critical or chronic illness and the possibility of finding a cure offering continued quality of life that gives you the optimum chance to choose living over dying.

- Receiving the best medical care and advice during the diagnostic stage of the illness.
- Being offered choices and options as to possible treatment, whether it be traditional, alternative, experimental or holistic.
- **Having the money** that will be needed to pay for the care should you be uninsured, or your health insurance carrier denies payment for the cost of the recommended treatment.
- **Being in control of your destiny**; not Congress, the President, or the Supreme Court.

If you don't have the money you don't have the control. It's that simple. Living Benefits Life Insurance provides access to the money, and therefore the power to control your and your family's destiny in the event of serious, even catastrophic illness, *before* it happens.

Living Benefits offers the freedom to choose life.

For nearly fifty years I have worked in the insurance and financial service industry on projects and solutions in which I believe deeply. A few years ago I was introduced to a concept called ***Living Benefits.*** It has already helped thousands of families and small business owners survive financially, and will continue to help many thousands more in the ensuing years.

It has provided the money necessary to fund the treatment and enormous expense of choosing life over death. It makes living instead of dying a possibility.

It is my privilege to share the *living benefits* story with you.

Richard Drazien – September 2012

Introduction

I wrote *No One Ever Told Me* because there is an unsettling exposure to a risk that could undermine the financial survival of over half of America's adult population. To a large extent that danger is going unaddressed by those in a position to know better.

Most foreclosures and bankruptcies are caused when individuals and families faced with a chronic or critical illness (stroke, heart attack, or diagnosis of cancer) are unable pay the extraordinarily high medical bills being incurred. You might assume this is an issue only for those who have no health or medical insurance. But most U.S. bankruptcies are filed by individuals who had health insurance which either did not come close to paying the high cost of their medical expenses or did not cover the treatment recommended.

Few financial planning professionals know or understand the predicament, therefore, are not aware of a possible solution. Their clients suffer because the problem and its resolution are not being identified. That can no longer continue to be the case.

If there is a solution to this problem that allows individuals and families to prepare to weather the storm *in advance of its arrival*, it needs to be brought to the attention of the public now.

That is my mission!

The answer is both smart and easy to understand. It receives tax favored treatment and addresses a disturbing problem with an affordable solution. Perhaps even better, it gives control to you, not to the government.

It needed a visionary to take existing IRS approved "moving parts," piece them together to build a financial engine that delivers real-world answers, and then find one or two insurance companies to say "we think you're right, it makes sense, and we'll develop it with you."

It now exists, and my objective is to share it with you so that you and your family might survive the *"what if"* financial consequences of serious illness that hovers over us like a dark cloud. I want you to have the quality of life and peace of mind you deserve, and the opportunity to pursue whatever traditional, holistic, or alternative medical treatment or procedure that will allow you to keep living your best life, and hopefully find a cure.

Though it varies for each of us, when you reach a certain age there are several real concerns that dominate our thoughts regarding quality of life and peace of mind. They help us to define our financial objectives and uncover tactics available to attain those goals. The methods may vary but the concerns are universal:

- Money (Accumulating enough; growing it; and keeping it safe)
- Health (Surviving a major illness financially and emotionally)
- Legacy (Having loved ones endure financially after you are gone)

I visited with Dr. Victor A. Puleo Jr. PhD., associate professor of Insurance, Finance, and Risk Management at the University of Central Arkansas and asked him to describe the ingredients needed in a financial vehicle to make it virtually perfect for addressing these issues. After considerable thought he named the following features:

1. *A significant tax-free benefit paid to a spouse or family member upon their death.*
2. *The ability to access needed funds for any reason in the event of critical, chronic, or terminal illness, regardless of age and with no credit check required, especially if they had lost their job and/or their health insurance.*
3. *A guarantee that the vehicle will allow one to build a tax-free retirement with:*
    - *No loss of principle or of previous earnings in a down market*
    - *Participation in the gain during an up market*
4. *The option to continue the plan in the event of a disability*
5. *It had to be easily understood, offer total safety, and be affordable.*

These five ingredients would be crucial in creating a *Living Benefits* strategy for survival. If someone had the vision to build such a living benefits package, it could ensure stability, peace of mind, security and a dreamed about quality of life for millions of American families. Surely, someone thinking differently about how to develop a solution to this universal puzzle has put together all the necessary moving parts in one perfect vehicle so that all five objectives could be attained. What would Steve Jobs have created if he were in the insurance and financial services business? I went looking and found it!

The movie, *Field of Dreams* taught us "if you build it, they will come." I wrote *No One Ever Told Me* to share what I discovered because *Living Benefits* will help offer your loved ones the financial ability and sustenance to continue life's journey. It is nothing short of a miracle and not sharing it would have been a flagrant error in judgment on my part.

Now you will never have to tell anyone that *no one ever told you.*

Chapter 1

Life Happens

As life happens, we often face events that were not anticipated. Some of them seem unlikely, or flat out remote. They rarely qualify for a *"what do I do if"* analysis.

Some events are most often dealt with ***when*** they happen. For example, a hurricane or tornado warning motivates us to evacuate when it is about to occur, not weeks, or months before hand. You can take precautionary steps such as reinforced building materials and generators to keep power on. But if it is a Category 4 or 5 Storm, you're going to hit the road and leave town.

Some events or crisis's are dealt with ***after*** they happen because you could not plan for them. Losing your job because the company downsized or was sold without any advance warning is an example.

The purpose of this book is to identify proven risk management principles and new planning techniques that can be put in place to help you and your family survive certain financial emergencies ***before*** they occur, not after. Should the *"what if"* never cross your path, you will have attained the *just in case* peace of mind you were seeking, and perhaps the ability to create a tax free retirement. My intent is to introduce the latest risk management concepts and strategies that exist in the marketplace.

But as is often the case with new and innovative solutions, many professionals in the financial planning field, and ***therefore their clients***, have not been introduced to them and remain simply unaware of their existence. It is that concern which mandated the *No One Ever Told Me* title of this book regardless of your being a financial planner, or more critically, the consumer. These are the five words you *never* want to say to your family, or to your clients, if you are the professional adviser responsible for their financial welfare.

I am not going to "overwhelm" you with unnecessary facts and figures meant to hit you over the head and scare you with OMG statistics. I don't like that approach and neither should you when we already know that critical illness events really do happen to a majority of people during their lifetime, and the repercussions are often devastating.

The ingredients you will need for survival are: (a) great medical advice, (b) choices, and (c) the money to pay for the recommended treatments you choose.

So that you will not have to worry about how to access the money you may require, I am going to show you how you can have it available before you might ever need it.

I'll ask meaningful *what if* questions for those seeking guidance, intelligent solutions, affordable choices, and real-world answers that provide peace of mind and security for their families by diminishing the negative financial impact of certain events.

No One Ever Told Me is a risk management guide for living!

Chapter 2

Managing the Risk

Risk can be defined as a state of uncertainty where some of the possibilities involve a catastrophic loss, or other undesirable outcome. The notion of risk implies a choice that would have had an influence on the outcome prior to the loss occurring.

Risk management is the identification of risk and the resulting insecurity that looms over our objectives. It seeks to identify resources that would minimize the impact of unforeseen events. Risks that come from uncertainty in financial markets, or of unpredictable cause such as severe chronic or critical illness, are the focus of this book.

Strategies to manage risk include reducing the negative effect of the risk, accepting some or all of the potential consequences of a particular risk, or perhaps best of all, transferring the risk to another party. Some methods used are:

1. Assess the vulnerability of your critical assets to specific threats
2. Determine the expected consequences of specific attacks on assets by that risk
3. Identify ways to reduce those risks based on a sound strategy

Risk management should:

- Create value and be part of decision making
- Be structured based on the best available information
- Be dynamic, and responsive to change
- Be capable of continual improvement and enhancement
- Be continually re-assessed

Insurance is a form of risk management primarily used to hedge against the risk of an uncertain loss. It is defined as the transfer of risk and potential loss, from one entity to another, in exchange for payment. An insurer is a company selling the insurance; the insured, or policyholder, is the person or entity buying the insurance policy. The practice of appraising and controlling risk is called Risk Management and we do it every day of our lives.

The transaction involves the insured assuming a relatively small loss in the form of premium payments to the insurer in exchange for their promise to compensate the insured in case of a financial loss. The insured receives an insurance policy which details the conditions and circumstances under which they will be financially compensated.

Virtually every major Fortune 500 Company has a Risk Management department.

But in your world, who is going to act as the risk manager should certain severe financial and emotional *what if* events impact you and your family, threatening to destroy everything you have worked so hard to achieve?

Ultimately that responsibility will fall to you.

Chapter 3

Why This Book?

Virtually everyone reading this knows **someone** (*a relative, friend, neighbor, business associate or co-worker*) who has experienced a serious illness themselves or with a family member. It may have been what is often referred to as a ***critical illness*** (think stroke, heart attack, or diagnosis of cancer), or a ***chronic illness*** requiring long term care due to the inability to perform two of the six activities of daily living (bathing, eating, continence, dressing, toileting and transferring), or an illness that can be defined as ***terminal.***

Our focus in *No One Ever Told Me* will be on critical and chronic illness for two reasons: (1) the likelihood of it occurring is so high and (2) you will likely survive and live many years. But with medical expenses so costly, I was not surprised to discover that the high price of becoming seriously ill was overwhelmingly responsible for most U.S. bankruptcies, and most of these individuals *had* health insurance. Can you even imagine what it is like if you had *no* coverage?

Should it happen to you or a member of your immediate family, how do you deal with the emotional and financial stress it causes? Life goes on. The bills keep coming. Your credit worthiness is damaged. Will the "*what if's*" come home to roost? What would you do? Here are a few of the issues that speak to the serious illness concern:

- What if you are unable to work? What will be your source of income?
- If your spouse is a stay-at-home parent will they need to find work?
- What if your spouse has to cut back their work schedule to provide care? Will the loss of income be significant?
- If you still have health insurance, is it going to cover your treatment and the cost? What if it does not?

- What if there is no health insurance coverage in place? How do you pay?
- What if you have *life insurance* for when you die, but no *long-term care* coverage or *critical illness* policy? How will you provide the support funding which often needs to be sustained for long periods of time?
- What if you cannot afford the premiums for three different policies?
- If you have adequate savings earmarked for retirement, can you afford to use up those funds to pay the costs associated with serious illness?
- Can you continue paying college tuition for your children?
- What if you can no longer afford the mortgage payments and are facing the threat of foreclosure?
- What if you've maxed out your credit cards and can't qualify for a loan?
- What if bankruptcy appears to be your only option?

These are all reasonable "real-world" questions and the answer boils down to your needing **money for survival now**, especially if loss of income has damaged your credit and ability to get a loan. "How do I do that" you ask? As Cuba Gooding said to Tom Cruise in the movie *Jerry McGuire,* "show me the money." That is this books intent!

Chapter 4

Why is What You Will Learn Important?

1. Most of us feel responsible for the financial well-being of those we love.
2. Most of us understand the concept of risk, and the need do the best we can to "manage" it by minimizing the impact its occurrence might have in the lives our family members. For example, if the weather report called for a mixture of sustained rain, sleet, snow, or ice over the next 30 days, and the tires on our primary vehicles were going bald, we would likely replace most if not all of them.
3. *No One Ever Told Me* should be mandatory reading in any *Life Happens course*.
4. If you thought it likely that you would be faced with one or more of the following potential risks what would you have donc:?

    - Dying too soon.
    - Having a stroke, heart attack or a diagnosis of cancer that would lead to an extended period of life with little or no money.
    - Needing long term care (LTC) due to the inability to perform two of the six activities of daily living that define qualifying for long term care.
    - Seeing your investment savings for retirement such as your 401K plan lose much of its value as happened in the last Wall Street financial meltdown.
5. If it had been possible, would you have insured *in advance* against some, or all of these risks?
6. Does it make sense to pay costly premiums for three or four different policies to insure against thcsc risks or would it bc more cost effective to have all the risks covered in one policy

that was within your means? If your answer is "one policy" this booklet will provide a strategy and smart solution.

- You will learn where the answers to your basic questions can to be found?
- You will learn if there is an affordable planning concept that will address this need for "living benefits"?
- You will learn if there is such a thing as insurance for ***living,*** not just for dying, and how to find out about it?
- You will discover where you can view actual people and their families who have faced critical illness, and survived, discuss how they financially prepared in advance using these *living benefit* strategies?

But since such things do happen in our lives, the ultimate "why this is important" reason is to avoid the unwelcome possibility of facing your loved ones with despair and saying "I wish someone had told me about *living benefits* sooner."

Chapter 5

Do You Really Need Critical Illness Coverage?

In 2009 the Center for Disease Control (CDC) reported that 3 out of 4 people (75%) over the age of 40 will experience a critical illness in their lifetime. That *is* an OMG number.

The simple answer to our question is "yes" because you are going to likely outlast a critical illness (heart attack, cancer, or stroke) for an extended period of time. But as mentioned earlier, survival comes with a good news / bad news scenario. Advances in medical and emergency care allow more people than ever to survive a critical illness prior to retirement. That's the good news, but only if you have the funds to pay for the recommended care.

The bad news is that although the majority of these individuals had health insurance, most experienced high deductibles, co-insurance payments, and prescriptions that are no longer covered, but costing hundreds of dollars each month. Some will want to seek alternative treatments or fly to get care at some out-of-state, or even out of country medical facility that has been recommended, but is not a covered expense.

While you are recovering, you're not working. But that doesn't stop the need to pay your mortgage, utilities, car payments, your life and health insurance premiums, and even the grocery bill.

Or the ultimate horror, you have no health insurance.

Critical illness (CI) coverage is very expensive as a stand alone individual policy purchase. And while some carriers will "allow" you to add a critical illness rider to their life insurance policy, it often increases your premium as much as double, making it unaffordable. The result is that few have critical illness coverage in their portfolio.

The obvious conclusion is that if so many of us over age 40 will suffer a critical illness, and we cannot afford to buy coverage for the risk, someone needed to" think differently" about creating a "smart" solution that addresses the problem.

I now know that a strategy truly exists and is available to nearly all of us if we take action ***before*** the risk event lands on our doorstep. It's the freedom to choose life.

That is the passion that motivated the writing of this book.

Chapter 6

OK, You Have My Attention. Show Me The Money!

Since the likelihood of needing critical or chronic care is so remarkably high, why has the only *traditional* solution been the purchase of a stand alone LTC and/or critical illness policy offering coverage at a costly premium? Consumers want real and better choices!

Overwhelmingly, they have chosen not to spend the additional money, thereby leaving themselves and their families exposed to these risks causing them to self-insure.

The obvious solution would be to have someone create and structure a life insurance policy in an actuarially sound manner, so that the face amount (death benefit) could be accessed (accelerated) as a living benefit in the event of a chronic or critical illness without waiting for the insured to die.

They could simply "accelerate" the death benefit by providing a *living benefit* feature, without any extra premium charge, if the insured desired to take advantage of the provision. I don't want to enroll you in actuarial class, but if no living benefit claim is made, the insurance company would pay the face amount at death. If there was a living benefit claim and they paid part of the death benefit in advance they would still pay a discounted portion of the unused face amount at time of death.

Couldn't this type of living benefit be **included** in virtually every life policy that the carrier sold (even inexpensive Term Life coverage) with no additional premium if only they would think differently about creating solutions? Makes sense, right?

I call the solution **Living Benefits Life Insurance** simply because most people, even if they own or are in the market for life insurance, will tell you that they are more concerned about their quality of life while they are living rather than dying.

Here are three individuals and their families who provide living proof of my theory. You'll meet them later in Chapter 17.

- Ronald Webb, a 52 year-old painter diagnosed with lung cancer.
- Sophia Dudley, a 38 year-old school teacher who one month after giving birth suffered three heart attacks while shopping in her local Wall-Mart and needed triple by-pass surgery to survive.
- Elliot Butler, a physician's assistant with a wife and three children, two of whom were in college, who suffered a heart attack requiring a stent implant.

Each had purchased life insurance from an agent to take care of their family in case of premature death. But they didn't die. Instead, they had a critical illness event and lived! Their goal was to recover and get well. They wanted the best medical care possible regardless of the cost. They were worried about losing income and no longer being able to pay their bills or meet their obligations. They did not want to drown financially. They'd need a ***living*** benefit, not a death benefit. Each of their families wanted Ronald, Sophia, and Elliot to live, not to die so they might receive a death benefit check.

Each had a policy with a face amount death benefit between $250,000 and $750,000, but needed financial assistance now. If they had owned the "old" type of *traditional* life insurance protection without living benefits, their financial advisor would have sent a nice "*Thinking About You - Get Well Soon*" card, perhaps with a box of candy.

Fortunately their agent had thought differently about his/her responsibility to help solve problems that might occur in real life to their clients. They had embraced the "new" type of coverage.

A *living benefit* claim was made not long after the coverage was in place and each agent hand delivered a "lifesaver" check of $80,000 for Ron; $120,000 for Sophia; and $100,000 for Elliot followed by an *additional* $100,000 shortly thereafter.

In a properly structured Living Benefit Life Insurance policy, future coverage does not terminate in the event of a critical or chronic illness claim. A reduced death benefit continues in force because a portion of it was accelerated to pay the claim. And that reduction in death benefit is accompanied by a *lowering of future premiums.*

Chapter 7

Let's Do the Math

They say a picture is worth a thousand words. Sometimes "numbers" are worth a bunch of pictures. For my example, I chose a male age 47 in excellent health (the professor referred to in the introduction). I knew he would be as interested as you in seeing the cost comparison for two reasons: (1) To make sure I was being accurate (he is a professor), and (2) He was considering the strategy being illustrated for his own insurance portfolio. *(He subsequently purchased the coverage).*

I illustrated three choices for him, all featuring proposals submitted by well known, highly-rated companies that are considered leaders in the industry. My purpose is not to sell or promote any insurance company product so company names are not mentioned. It is to simply illustrate a concept that is neither well publicized nor understood by "experts" who should know better. It is available in the marketplace, and has already helped thousands of families survive the unexpected.

The usual reaction after reviewing the comparison is "You've got to be kidding. Why didn't I know about this?" But I am serious and now you'll know why!

Male Age 47 – Excellent Health

Choice 1 – Purchase two separate individual policies

Policy Type	Coverage	Monthly Premium
Long Term Care 5% Inflation compounding	$5,000 per month 90 day wait – 48 months	$111.68
Critical Illness	$250,000 Lump Sum	$224.88
No life insurance	-0-	-0-
TOTAL Premium		**$336.56 per month**

Choice 2 – Purchase three separate policies including life insurance

Policy Type	Coverage	Monthly Premium
Long Term Care 5% Inflation compounding	$5,000 per month 90 day wait – 48 months	$111.68
Critical Illness	$250,000 Lump Sum	$224.88
Term Life Insurance	$500,000 - 20 year level	$79.00
TOTAL Premium		**$415.56 per month**

Choice 3 – Purchase one life policy with Living Benefits included

Policy Type	Coverage	Monthly Premium
Term Life Insurance With Living Benefits Chronic Illness (LTC)	$500,000 20 year level rate guarantee $5,000 approx. per month increasing (based on illustration) 90 day wait – 45 months	
Critical Illness	$300,000 approx.* (based on illustration)	

*Based on severity of claim, age at time of claim, and impact on life expectancy

TOTAL MONTLY PREMIUM	**$108.94** (Includes all coverage)

Are you with me so far?

Chapter 8

What Do the Numbers Tell Us?

In Choice 1 the client purchased two separate contracts; a $5,000 per month for 4 years long-term care policy with a monthly premium of $111.68 per month and a $250,000 critical illness policy with a monthly premium of $224.88. **The total monthly payment was $336.56**. He did not have a life insurance policy. If he died never having had a critical (CI) or chronic (LTC) claim, his beneficiary (family or business partner) received nada, nothing, zip, zilch.

In Choice 2 we illustrated the client purchasing the same two separate policies, but in addition he already had in place a $500,000 20-year level term life policy to protect his family when he died. That policy added another $79 per month bringing his **total monthly premium outlay to $415.56.** *That's a lot of money.*

Not too exciting so far, but wait.

In Choice 3 the 47 year old male client purchases a $500,000 guaranteed 20-year level term policy that includes an accelerated death benefit *living benefits* rider which allows the insured access to a portion of his face amount (death benefit) in the event of a chronic, critical, or terminal illness occurrence as defined in the contract. Simply put, the insurance company "accelerates" the death benefit and willingly lets the insured access a portion of it if they choose to do so. Once the claim is approved, no one, and certainly not the insurance company, can tell you how to spend the money or has the right to approve any treatments you may wish to pursue.

Now for the amazing part…
The guaranteed 20-year level premium for the **$500,000 Living Benefits Life Insurance policy** which includes significant protection in the event of a chronic illness *(think long-term care),* a critical illness

(*think stroke, heart attack, or cancer diagnosis),* or a terminal illness is only… **$108.94 per month.**

That is $227 less each month than Choice 1.
That is $306 less each month than Choice 2.

This is so powerful for the security of your family that I will rephrase the benefit:

- Instead of paying $336 per month in Choice 1 (and having no life insurance), the client could choose the Living Benefits strategy (Choice 3) and **saved $227 per month.** And not only did he save the $227, if he never had a serious illness claim while living, his named beneficiary would receive a $500,000 income tax free payment upon his death.

- or -

- Instead of paying $415 per month for the coverage in Choice 2 which is the same as Choice 1 but includes the premium already being paid for an existing life insurance policy, the client could purchase Choice 3 and **save $306 each and every month.**

Note: What I have illustrated works for any age or gender

The Living Benefit Choice gets even better:

- If the client prefers Choice 3, but desires **a 30 year level premium guarantee** instead of 20 years, his premium would be $172 per month instead of $108. Still a fraction of the cost for Choice 1 or 2.
- In Choice 1 and 2, the premiums for the long term care and critical illness coverage are not guaranteed. The insurer has granted itself the contractual right to raise them under certain circumstances, such as poor claims experience. I call it the "*we don't really want to offer this insurance anymore*" provision. I think you'll agree that **a 20 or 30 year guarantee that the premium cannot increase is a better idea for your peace of mind!**
- Can you add an optional Disability Waiver of Premium provision that requires the insurer to continue paying your premium in the event you become disabled as contractually described in the policy? Yes you can!

Chapter 9

Long-Term Care Coverage and Living Benefits Life Insurance

In 2012 it is estimated that about 9 million Americans over the age of 65 will need long-term care services. That number is expected to increase to 12 million in 2020 and the cost of care may be as much as $4,000 to $8,000 per month (1). Unfortunately, Medicare and private health insurance plans will not pay for the majority of services that most people need. Medicare will only pay for a maximum of 100 days in a nursing home and will not pay for any home health or adult day care (2). And the needed services cost the person who needs the chronic care a small fortune. If they do not have the money, or deplete what they had set aside, the financial responsibility and burden of providing quality of care most likely fall to the spouse and children. It's a nightmare.

Yet only 5-6% of our aging population owns a long-term care (LTC) policy because: *(2)*

- *Traditional stand alone LTC policies are very expensive*
- *Underwriting is more difficult because it is based on morbidity (illness), not mortality (death), therefore, pre-existing conditions may often be declined*
- *The cost of coverage is subject to rate increases, sometimes doubling the premium*
- *Dying without ever having had a claim and receiving nothing creates a "Use it or lose it / I didn't get my moneys worth" mindset*
- *Benefits are typically paid as a reimbursement of expenses with likely restrictions*

And there is more bad news. The long-term care insurance business has not been financially rewarding to the LTC carriers and they are leaving the business in droves. Ten of the 20 largest companies have stopped offering long-term care coverage, with Prudential and MetLife the most recent to run for the hills (3).

But for those who paid attention to the premium costs in the three choices given to our 47 year old client, you may have already spotted more good news:

- The premium of $111.68 per month for *just* the long-term care policy is MORE than the $108.94 total monthly premium for the Living Benefits Choice #3 which INCLUDED all of these features:

    - $500,000 of 20 year tem life insurance.
    - Access to an accelerated lump sum critical illness benefit of approximately $300,000 (advanced from the face amount of the policy) without restrictions on how the money is used.
    - $5,000 per month long-term care benefit for 45 months with no restrictions on usage.
    - Elimination of the "if you don't use it you lose it" factor.
    - If the insured dies without ever making a claim his beneficiary would receive a $500,000 income tax free death benefit instead of nothing.

By choosing Choice 3 the insured did not need to spend an additional $111 on a LTC policy because chronic illness coverage was already part of his Living Benefits program.

(1) www.longtermcare.gov
(2) www.limra.com
(3)Life Health Pro Magazine – April 9, 2012 "Looking for Long-Term Care Coverage? You might not find it."

Chapter 10

Double Down

Let's do some more simple mathematics though I suspect a number of you are already ahead of me on this one. I call it "doubling down."

What if our 47 year-old, upon reviewing his family and business obligations and circumstances, concluded that he needed more life insurance? Let's say that he, his estate planning attorney, and his financial planning team thought **$1 Million** was the right amount of insurance for him to carry.

By doubling the coverage in Choice 3 his monthly premium would increase to $216.

Our 47 year-old is *still* spending a good deal less per month than in Choice 1 or 2 ($120 or $200 less respectively) but *now* has $1,000,000 of income tax free life insurance if there is a named beneficiary.

In our example the chronic illness (LTC) and/or critical illness (CI) claim maximum accelerated payout has **increased to $500,000**. As before, the full death benefit (face amount) will be discounted by any living benefit claim payments previously accessed by the insured.

Should the 47 year-old insured prefer that the $1,000,000 policy have a *30 year* level rate guarantee his premium would be $342 per month, virtually the same as Choice 1 which has NO life insurance, and *still* $73 per month less than Choice 2.

Chapter 11

I Always Thought Life Insurance was Just for Dying.

For readers who are not in the life insurance business please indulge me as I take you on a *brief* journey of the history of life insurance so you can appreciate the evolution of the living benefit plus tax-free retirement concept, its simple brilliance, and the nature of its inherent tax advantages. In the spirit of keeping you awake, I will attempt to make it as interesting as possible by avoiding actuarial mumbo jumbo.

The concept of life insurance as a benefit to society is at least 180 years old. Its purpose was to allow the family to continue to survive financially after the death of the bread winner without becoming dependent on help from the government, friends, and society in general. It was meant to encourage us to take care of our own so that the burden did not shift to others. And yes, at the beginning it was just for dying.

In structure the element of risk, i.e., the likelihood of dying, was based upon age. The older you were the more it would cost. The insurer also took into consideration the health and likely longevity of the insured in determining the premium. That has never changed, with the exception of a more sophisticated procedure for gathering medical history and information. Since I was not around 180 years ago I can only guess it worked like this: You chose an amount of coverage, then gave your date of birth, and answered a few "health" questions posed by the sales agent. You then were told the cost for 12 months worth of life insurance. On your next birthday you received a renewal opportunity at higher premium for the next year due to your being one year older.

Today that would be called an annually renewable term life policy. The attraction was that it was cost effectivc (chcap) for that onc- ycar period. If you lived for the year you received no benefit, just the opportunity to do it again for one more year. The problem was that as you became older the premium would escalate each year, often to the point when, 10, 20 or 30 years later you could no longer afford to pay next years cost. If you didn't die the insurance company kept all the money you paid in. You got back nothing. They bet that you would live a long time and die after you stopped paying premiums. Sounds callous, but it's hard to argue with their reasoning.

"Solutions" to this problem were developed over the years.

1. Offering term life with a guarantee level premium for a selected number of years, i.e., 10, 20, 25, 30-year term, or longer. If you were age 30, you could perhaps buy a level premium term policy until age 65. Seems reasonable, but if you kept the policy to the end of the level premium period, your rate upon renewal went through the roof, to the point that one would only renew if on their death bed. Again, the insurance company was betting that you would die *after* the policy had lapsed. To be fair, we're not picking on them because it is possible that the insured could die in the first year of the policy. But much like Vegas the house (company) has the law of large numbers on their side.

2. Offering a "permanent" Whole Life policy with a guaranteed level premium to age 95 or 100, or even 120 (you should only live so long). That was accomplished by "averaging" the premium cost over an extended age period, so that if you were 40 years old at time of purchase you would be paying the same level premium at age 40 as you would at age 80 or 90.

The key to understanding the nature of all "permanent" life insurance policies, is that you are "overpaying" for the risk you are insuring against (death) at the beginning so that you will be able to keep it in force until the end. The rationale is that paying the same at the start as at the end makes it likely that you will have the "whole life" insurance protection in effect whenever you die, thereby making it permanent. Are you still awake?

In addition to keeping your premium level, Whole Life offers the additional benefit of a growing cash value account giving you "credit" for paying more than required to cover the risk in the early policy years. The extra premiums you pay early are set aside in a cash value account that "belongs" to you. The death benefit still passes income tax free to your named beneficiary as it does in term insurance, but to make it more attractive **the cash value account grows in a tax deferred manner and can later be withdrawn tax free**. The IRS likes this because it shifts the burden of responsibility for the welfare of your loved ones from them (government) to you.

The growth of the cash value may have been tax deferred and safe, but it provided a ***very*** conservative return. Slow and steady may win a turtle race, but the prime interest rate hovered in double digit territory for nearly six years (1978 – 1984) reaching a high of 20.5% in July of 1981. In comparison Whole Life looked old, boring, inflexible, and behind the times. So, solution number three is born.

3. In order to compete, the life insurance industry needed a game changer. They called it Universal Life (UL). A lot of the features incorporated in traditional Universal Life were good. It was flexible, even allowing the insured to increase or *decrease* the premium from year to year (within contractual and actuarial guidelines) as their circumstances changed. But timing is everything, and for the UL contract, timing was bad. With UL the insurance company could "project," but not guarantee performance based on then current interest rates. You can see the problem coming. An agent could very well order a proposal *projecting* the current 13-14% interest rate into the future... even forever, and inadvertently *forget* to tell the client that interest rates may fall. The client had come away believing that these hypothetical projections would last forever. But it was merely an illustration of the possible, not necessarily the likely. And when they did fall, the policies imploded unless the insured paid in more premium than they had anticipated. Not a pretty picture.

So while the interest rates were going south, the stock market was heading skyward. In an attempt to tie the returns of the life policy to the equity market a second variation of Universal Life was created.

4. It was called Variable Universal Life (VUL). But since the return within the policy is based on stock market performance, both positive and negative, all of us have learned through experience that what goes up can also come down. When the bubble bursts, the slippery slope down can become frightening. I will not spend any more time on VUL other than what is obvious. Instead of the cash value growth being less than projected in the traditional UL, it could actually decrease (lose value) in the VUL structure. Not good if the market is going in the wrong direction for a long time.

You can accuse the life insurance industry of being conservative to a fault, or too quick to jump on the latest hot trend. But some of them are fast learners because the UL and VUL experience provided them with the answer. Take the best of each concept, eliminate the worst case scenario, blend them together, and you are guaranteed to make magic.

5. This ultimate blend is called **Indexed** Universal Life (IUL) and in my opinion, is the one perfect product (*I prefer the word engine*) to address the most serious financial issues being faced by American families and small businesses. To be considered faultless it needed to not just address, but to come as close as possible to guaranteeing financial survival of the family in the event of:

    - Another economic meltdown affecting savings and retirement accounts
    - An increase in income taxes
    - The need to access a meaningful amount of money to help pay the often exorbitant costs associated with critical illness, chronic illness, and terminal illness
    - Death

Here are just four of the many features which make **Indexed Universal Life** so special:

- Total protection from market loss because the policy guarantees that your cash value will **never, ever, have a negative return.**
- An annual reset provision allowing you to ***lock in*** each year of positive return so that the policy cash value growth can never be lost due to negative market performance.
- A "capped" participation in the growth index that your policy is tracking. No downside and participation in the upside is contractually guaranteed. It doesn't get much better than that.
- In many states, the cash value accumulated inside the life insurance policy is protected from creditors in the event of bankruptcy, judgments, or lawsuits, malpractice or other wise. (Doctors and business owners love this feature).

Please make sure you check the law in your state.

Chapter 12

What's for Dessert?

Yes, there is icing on the cake. In the Introduction that began the book, I listed five features that the Professor said were necessary and must be included in order to make the strategy and vehicle being driven, virtually perfect? The third one was:

A guarantee that the vehicle will allow one to build a tax-free retirement with:

- **No loss of principle or of previous earnings in a down market**
- **Participation in the gain during an up market**

Put another way, a guarantee that:

1. You will never lose money no matter what the market does, not ever!
2. Not only do you participate in the gain if the market goes up, but you will never lose the gain, even in down market years.
3. The money will grow tax-deferred and can be withdrawn tax-free.

The LIVING BENEFITS Insurance Strategy that I have described can ***also*** be structured to become a totally safe tax-free retirement program, i.e., Living Benefits in case of serious illness AND a Tax-Free Retirement, all combined in ONE affordable package? **That is truly ground breaking!**

We will dedicate the next Chapter to tax free retirement and examine why so few professional financial planners and insurance agents know about, or understand it, and as a result, never told you because they couldn't.

But now YOU know!!!

Chapter 13

Creating a Tax-Free Retirement

As introduced in Chapter 11 and expanded upon in Chapter 12, the most revolutionary feature of Living Benefits Life Insurance may very well be the ability to attain two of your most sought after objectives in one product solution. Let me make this crystal clear. If you choose to use the Universal Life engine (Traditional or Indexed) instead of the Term Insurance engine, you have put in place the ability to financially survive a critical illness event AND to establish a safe **Tax–Free Retirement (TFR) plan.**

With one strategy, one premium commitment, and complete control, you can achieve virtually all of your goals, no matter what obstacles are put in your path along life's journey. Here are just a few of the advantages:

- There are no government or IRS regulations dictating how much money you can set aside in your Indexed Universal Life (IUL) contract
- You do not have to include employees in your TFR plan.
- The increasing cash value account grows in a tax deferred manner.
- There are no government retirement age restrictions as to when you can begin withdrawing income without penalty.
- The insurance policy contains provisions allowing you income tax-free access to your cash value account, no matter what Congress does to tax rates.
- A significant income tax-free death benefit paid to your named beneficiary that avoids probate and, depending on ownership, may also be estate tax-free.
- Safety, safety, safety!

- Access to a portion of the death benefit in the event of a qualifying chronic or critical illness with no restrictions on how you use the money. But that can ONLY happen if your Universal Life policy INCLUDES the living benefit provisions we have talked about.

Let me repeat that last one.

To have **both** a tax-free retirement AND access to meaningful funds in case of a chronic, critical, or terminal illness the traditional or indexed Universal Life policy **MUST INCLUDE THE LIVING BENEFITS** contractual provision. Please keep in mind that the overwhelming amount of life insurance sold in America does NOT i**nclude** a comprehensive living benefits provision. You will need it if you wish to provide your family with both of the benefits.

The individual who introduced you to this book is best positioned to explain the details of this concept, provide a personalized illustration, and answer your questions about the features, benefits, and safety built into the tax-free retirement strategy discussed herein.

Chapter 14

Peace of Mind Declaration

Now that you know the history of the life insurance policy and its pedigree you can appreciate why it is the perfect vehicle to accommodate all moving parts necessary to provide solutions to the issues we have posed. And it can be accomplished with security, safety, and trust.

If I had to sum up what is the central theme of *No One Ever Told Me* my answer would be it is about "***Achieving Peace of Mind***". We all want to pursue a quality of life that can be reached without stress. The song lyric, "don't worry, be happy" is a slight over simplification, but if we can reduce some of the "*what ifs*" that we worry about we get a lot closer to our goal. My passion for **combining *living benefits*** with the time tested tax advantaged benefits of life insurance has not wavered since I discovered it was possible to do so.

It is a classic example of the age old cliché, "the whole is larger than the sum of the parts."

To summarize, I took the three biggest concerns that cause us to lose sleep:

- Money (Accumulating enough; growing it; and keeping it safe)
- Health (Surviving a major illness financially and emotionally)
- Legacy (Having loved ones endure financially after you are gone)

Then I went in search of one cost effective strategy, concept, or product (which ever word you prefer) that would resolve at least two, but **preferably all three issues**.

Here is what I discovered:

1. A term life insurance policy which includes the *living benefits* ability to advance a portion of the face amount (death benefit) in the event of a qualifying serious illness claim should effectively deal with the Health and Legacy concerns sited above, depending on the premium guarantee period. Utilizing term life keeps the premiums remarkably affordable.
2. Depending on age, an Indexed Universal Life policy including *living benefits* provides the solution for ALL three objectives. The IUL "engine" offers access to the funds needed to survive a serious illness, without a credit check and without anyone telling you how to spend the money. It presents the beneficiary with an income tax- free legacy at the insured's death, and finally, lets your cash accumulation grow tax-deferred; lets you take it out tax-free at retirement, lets you contribute as much as you want without government rules and regulations, and most importantly you retain all gains and NEVER suffer a loss in value. How good is that?

... And even if you begin with Living Benefit Term (#1 above), you have the ability to convert it to the Indexed Universal model (#2).

Chapter 15

Life Insurance for LIVING! Why Have I Never Heard About This?

Most people purchase life insurance for the death benefit. For health and medical coverage they look to health insurance. Each has its own scientific risk management characteristics and statistical assumptions, *mortality* (death) for life insurance companies and *morbidity* (illness) for the health insurance providers.

The visionary concept of allowing the insured to access (accelerate) a portion of their life policy's death benefit in the event of a *severe or life threatening* chronic or critical illness is relatively new. The basic theory is simple. If you have a "terminal" illness (defined as no more than a year or two to live) the life insurance carrier is already looking at a pending death claim. So paying it a little early by slightly "discounting" the full face amount was a no-brainer. But allowing the insured, in cases of serious illness, to access a portion of the funds to continue living, perhaps find a cure, stay alive, and allow the family an opportunity to financially survive was a stroke of genius.

To answer the question posed in the title of this chapter, the insurance and financial service industry, especially its distribution system, is slow to embrace change. Life insurance agents are often challenged to understand and explain the complexity of the traditional products they offer. When something new and revolutionary comes along how are they going to hear about it? If they are a "captive" agent of a company that is complacent with what they market, they may never come in contact with the ***Life Insurance for Living*** concept. And if an overwhelming percentage of agents and financial planners in the industry don't know about it, how is the client's accountant, lawyer, or stock broker ever going to trip over it, much less understand it, and then tell you about it? Chances are slim to none.

A case in point came across my desk the other day. Two credentialed attorneys published an article in the April issue of *LifeHealthPro* magazine bemoaning the fact that it is becoming increasingly difficult to find long-term care coverage. Therefore "what do you tell your clients" they asked of the life/health agent reader? Their possible solution was a *long-term care annuity* which they acknowledge had a "small downside," namely that it required a lump sum investment of around $100,000. They are "professionals" who seemed *clueless* about a real-world solution, as described in this book, which makes substantial amounts of money available for chronic illness (long-term care), critical illness, as well as, at death.

Perhaps they would have rethought their article if they had the advantage of reading *No One Ever Told Me,* or visiting with the 47-year old client who packaged $500,000 of life insurance; $5,000 per month for long-term care; and $300,000 for critical illness into one financial vehicle for a total premium of $108 per month... and kept the $100,000 safe and growing wherever it was being held. You think?

It brings us full circle to a point made earlier. Even if you could afford to spend your own funds to pay for extensive medical care, why not transfer the risk to the insurance company and use their money, not yours?

They, and other so called *experts*, need to know more about the *living benefits* solution.

Chapter 16

I Own Life Insurance Without Living Benefits. What Should I Do?

There are several steps for you to consider.

The first is to determine what type of coverage you purchased (Term, Whole Life, or Universal Life), your age when purchased, the purpose, the cost, and your current health (has it changed).

Then you might ask the agent who sold you the policy or policies, if they were ***the old or new type of life insurance****?* If the former agent says "what do you mean" your reply is ***"Can I access a portion of the death benefit if I need long-term care or have a stroke, heart attack, or am diagnosed with cancer?***" If the answer is "I don't know," or "what are you talking about," or "no, this is life insurance for when you die, not health insurance," you do not have *Living Benefit Life Insurance.*

The industry refers to the "letting go" of existing life insurance in order to purchase a new policy as a "replacement" sale. They want to make sure that you understand the advantages as well as the disadvantages, if any. How do the policies really compare? Ultimately, it is always going to be about features and benefits.

The next step now that you know "living benefits" life insurance exists, is determining the importance of living benefits for financial survival if the health and market risks we have discussed actually occur to you or a family member.

And finally, if having "living benefits" seems to make sense and you would like to learn more about the features, benefits, and premium at your age, I would suggest you seek out a professional with the expertise to help you determine the value of "replacement" and whether or not it is in your family's interest. That expert is likely to be the person who introduced you to this book.

As we live longer because of medical breakthroughs and new found knowledge on how to take better care of ourselves, I am increasingly concerned that most of us are not prepared for the impact a critical or chronic illness would have on our family's emotional and financial survival. This is especially true if we continue living for extended periods of time without the financial ability to maintain the quality of life we had hoped for.

As a believer in the power of the idea and concept I have introduced to you, I cannot fathom why anyone would want life insurance without living benefits, especially after analyzing the numbers. I understand the "it's too good to be true" skepticism, but it is just not warranted in this situation.

If you are not sure how you came across *No One Ever Told Me,* I can help you locate an expert in your area who shares my passion for the concept. I will provide my contact details at the end of the book should you desire my help. I have been an independent financial service professional and consultant for nearly fifty years. I am not a licensed insurance agent and I do not share in commissions.

Chapter 17

Where Can I Learn More About Living Benefit Life Insurance??

Here are three sources:

1. If you received this book from a life insurancc and financial planning professional, he or she would be the person to explain how the living benefits concept might work for you. He or she will prepare several proposals to illustrate the flexibility and show you how to best adapt its features to your needs.

2. If you wish to view short videos featuring the three individuals and families referenced in Chapter 7 (the Webbs, Dudleys and Butlers) who had made living benefit critical illness claims, received substantial lump sum payments that helped them survive financially, and wanted to share their experience with others, please visit the Alliance Group website at http://anallianceforlife.com

   They are real people who tell the living benefits story better than I ever could. I have been privileged to meet one of the couples and to have visited with the financial professional who brought the concept to the attention of his client. As you can imagine, the experience of delivering the claim check was life changing for both the client and the representative.

3. If you are not sure how the book came into your hands, I suggest you go to the Alliance Group website shown above, contact them by email to receive more information, and perhaps request the name of a representative close to you.

4. If you are a representative of an agency, insurance company, or a financial institution that does not offer *living benefits*, visit the Alliance Group website, talk with the person who

introduced you to this book, or if you prefer, feel comfortable in contacting me. I'll do my best to lead you in the right direction.

5. If you are looking for a career change and have the passion to truly assist individuals, families, and small business owners prepare for some of the challenges placed in their path during life's journey, you may contact the Alliance Group as well. The experience will prove life changing for you and those you help.

If you wish to order additional copies of *No One Ever Told Me* please request them from the person who offered the book to you, email me at rickdraz@yahoo.com, or go to the Alliance Group web site at http://analliance forlife.com.

If you have any questions regarding the content or perspective taken in the book, the best way that I can be reached is by email.

Please remember that I am not a sales agent. My mission was to bring the concept of Living Benefit Life Insurance to your attention, and with that intent, comes the responsibility of answering your questions and providing additional guidance.

I would welcome the opportunity!

Chapter 18

Final Thought

I always appreciate a message that can be delivered with a powerful word picture or visual. There are approximately 500 Joseph A. Bank Clothing stores in 42 states, so many of you are familiar with how they distinguish and brand their marketing concept. They appear to be affordable and tuned in to what features will really appeal to their customer. They seem successful.

Recently I was strolling by one of their stores in Jacksonville, Florida and was stopped in my tracks by the following full window advertisement display:

BUY 1 SUIT – GET 2 MORE FREE

Thc visual was perfect. It featured three good looking suits with the tagline,

Pay for One and Get All Three

In perception, that's the ground breaking attraction of ***Living Benefits Life***. Purchase life insurance and receive critical illness & chronic illness (long-term care) coverage *free.*

Pay for one and get all three is a *concept.*

Insurance company actuaries and compliance officers might well have a heart attack or stroke reading this view and depiction of the *living benefits* concept, especially the metaphorical use of the word *free*.

But in the eyes of the beholder, *it is what it is!*

Like thousands of others, if the actuary or compliance officer did, heaven forbid, have a stroke or heart attack, I believe they would hope to be insured by a life policy with living benefits *included at no additional premium!*

Wouldn't you?

About the Author

Rick Drazien has nearly 50 years professional experience in the financial services industry, and is well versed in the history of the industry and the pedigree of various cutting edge products. In addition to developing a ***Senior Risk Manager*** (SRM) professional designation program and course of study, he was engaged as an independent consultant to New York Life in the late 90's to help them educate and train agents on a product they developed nationally for the late adult marketplace. His article, entitled ***Understanding the Late Adulthood and Senior Market*** was published in the March 2001 edition of the industry leading magazine, *Best's Review*.

At the request of the Florida Medical Association (FMA), he founded FMA Physicians Advantage in 2003 to act as their exclusively endorsed insurance and financial services division. Rick's mandate was to provide the best possible financial counsel to the 15,000 physician members of the FMA, with emphasis on medical malpractice asset protection. The result was his visionary development of the highly successful CAPS+ Comprehensive Asset Protection program for physicians. He retired as CEO of the company in 2006 to pursue his passion for creative writing.

In 2010 he met John Craft, Founder and CEO of the Alliance Marketing Group. It was the first time Rick had heard about the concept of ***including*** "living benefits" as a contractual feature of a life insurance policy without charging an additional premium. As John explained it, life insurance should be as much for living as for dying. *"Why couldn't you have a contractual provision in the policy to accelerate a portion of the death benefit and allow voluntary access to it if the insured has a qualifying chronic or critical illness?"*

And if it were available ***why would anyone choose not to have it as an included part of their life insurance policy?*** Rick still hasn't thought of a reason why not.

From his perspective, the miracle of ***living benefits life insurance*** is real, makes perfect sense, is easy to understand, cost effective, and most importantly, offers the peace of mind that the consumer is looking for. He continues to be grateful that someone took the time to think differently about resolving this critical "*what if*" issue for the thousands of American families and business owners who may confront this issue along life's journey.

He has also authored the well received and entertaining inspirational book:

"Because I Couldn't Kill My Frog"
A Guide to Mentoring and Finding Your Passion

If you wish to have Mr. Drazien speak to your group or organization, he can best be reached by email at rickdraz@yahoo.com.

ADDENDUM

Critical and Chronic Illness Statistical Reference

WHAT CAN HAPPEN TO YOU

HEART ATTACK

- About every 34 seconds, someone in the United States has a Myocardial infarction (heart attack).[1]

STROKE

- On average, a stroke occurs every 40 seconds.[2]

CANCER

- A new cancer is diagnosed every 30 seconds in the United States.[3]
- 1 in 2 men and women will be diagnosed with cancer in their lifetime.[4]

1. "About Heart Attacks" AHA 6/12/11. http://www.heart.org/HEARTORG/Conditions/HeartAttack/AboutHeartAttacks/About-Heart-Attacks_UCM_002038_Article.jsp (24 April 2012).
2. "Impact of Stoke" American Stoke Assoc. 18 April 2012. http://www.strokeassociation.org/STROKEORG/AboutStroke/Impact-of-Stroke_UCM_310728_Article.jsp (24 April 2012).
3. "Cancer Facts & the War on Cancer" National Cancer Institute. 2012. http://training.seer.cancer.gov/disease/war/ (24 April 2012).

4 "SEER Stat Fact Sheets: All Sites" National Cancer Institute. 2012. http://seer.cancer.gov/statfacts/html/all.html (25 April 2012).

CHANCE OF SURVIVAL

Heart Attack – 60%
Stroke – 70%
Breast Cancer – 87%
Prostate Cancer – 98%[1]

CHANCE OF FINANCIAL SURVIVAL

Nearly half of people whose families have been affected by cancer say the costs of cancer care were a burden on their family, including one in six who say such costs were a MAJOR burden.[2]

The cost of a severe heart attack – including direct and indirect costs – is about $1 million.[3]

1.5 million Americans will declare bankruptcy this year and 60% are due to medical bills.[4]

1. "Critical Illness Statistics" Pinney Insurance Center, 2012. http://www.pinneyinsurance.com/critical-illness/statistics.php (13 April 2012).
2. "National Survey of Households Affected by Cancer" USA Today/KFF/Harvard School of Pub. Health, November 2006. ttp://www.kff.org/kaiserpolls/upload/7591.pdf (13 April 2012).
3. Shaw LJ, Merz CNB, Pepine CJ, et al. The Economic Burden of Angina in Women with Suspected Ischemic Heart Disease: Results from the National Institutes of Health National Heart, Lung, and Blood Institute-Sponsored Women's Ischemia Syndrome Evaluation. Circulation. August 29, 2006 2006; 114(9):894-904.
4. "The Real Risk That You'll Have a Critical Illness" Facts about Critical Illness Insurance Coverage and Costs, 2012 http://www.criticalillnessinsuranceinfo.org/ (13 April 2012).

YOU MAY BECOME CHRONICALLY ILL

Chronic Illness affects many people and can create additional expenses for a family. Some of these expenses may include:

Nursing Home Cost for a Private Room

- For nursing home care, the national monthly average is currently $6,266, or $75,190 annually. [1]

Assisted Living Facility

- For assisted living facilities the national monthly avg is now $3,185, or $38,220 annually.[1]

Home Health Aide (Certified)

- The national monthly average cost for home health aide is $3,623 or $43,472 annually. [1]

1. "Cost of Care Survey" Genworth 2012. http://www.retirementguard.com/files/library/2010_Cost_of_Care_Survey_Full_Report.pdf (13 April 2012).

48 – 48 – 60 (WHAT THESE NUMBERS MEAN)

- 48% of mortgage foreclosures are a result of financial hardship due to Critical Illness (only 3% due to death).[1]
- 48% of businesses that fail are due to a critical illness.[2]
- 60% or more of all bankruptcies are directly tied to medical conditions such as critical illnesses, and around 80% of the individuals were already covered by health insurance.[3]

1. Get Sick, Get Out: The Medical Causes of Home Foreclosures" Health Matrix, 2008.
2. Goldstein, Mark, "Critical Illness Insurance 101" http://ezinearticles.com/?Critical-Illness-Insurance-101&id=4450375 (13 April 2012).
3. "More People are Surviving Critical Illnesses" US Critical Illness INS Resource CR, 2012. http://criticalillnesspolicies.com/insurance-coverage/critical-illness-statistics/ (13 April 2012).

Acknowledgements

At its heart, the essential ingredient for writing a non-fiction book that people may actually want to read is the passion of the author for the subject chosen, and why they believe it will benefit the reader. *No One Ever Told Me* gave me the opportunity to place a spotlight on a critical problem for millions of Americans during a time of economic upheaval and philosophical disagreement, and to introduce a concept that would provide a solution. Its core message is that we can and must take control of addressing the issue without hoping that someone else (government, politicians or industry) will do it for us if it suits their purpose. After numerous interviews it was evident that most understood the financial survival challenge of critical illness, but few were aware that the brilliantly designed *living benefits* solution existed.

To get it right, I needed help from many people. After the "final" draft is written someone has to proof read it to find all the typo's, the misspelling that spell check missed, the words that were unnecessary or just didn't belong where I put them, and the sentences that made no sense. Great thanks to my daughter, Lori Cowen, who diligently edited her father's work with tender love and care. And to Tegan Cutler of Premier Graphics, Julie Defoer of Good Eye Design and Chris Benzel, for making the book come to life and giving it eye appeal.

My gratitude goes to those who took the time to read the manuscript in it varying stages and helped to make it better. There were many, but a special shout out goes to Dr. Victor A. Puleo, Jr., CFP, Associate Professor of Insurance and Risk Management at the University of Central Arkansas for asking the hard questions and making sure he received the correct answer.

A sincere thank you to John Craft, CEO and co-Founder of the Alliance Group for his creative vision as part of the team that developed the *living benefits* concept, and for his always being available to provide answers to the questions I asked. And to Lee Duncan and Peter Goldfine of the Alliance Group who read the manuscript and did everything possible to make sure my facts, figures, and reference footnotes were accurate. Any misstatements or inaccuracies are solely the fault of the author.

I must also recognize the beautiful city of Bellingham, Washington where I spent the last three months finishing the manuscript. And heartfelt thanks to *Sibyl Stanford,* the internationally renowned watercolorist and author of *Painting the Spirit Within,* whose friendship my wife and I will forever treasure. As serendipity would have it, Sibyl was our next door neighbor in Bellingham and inspired us daily with her extraordinary kindness and grace. She read the manuscript and quietly offered some suggestions which were happily enacted by the author.

And most importantly I thank my amazing wife Carolyn, without whose patience, encouragement and unwavering support there is no book. She continually read each new version of the manuscript I placed before her, rolled her eyes, and then made it better. I love her to pieces and am grateful for having her at my side every day.